The CFORC Catechism

The Christian Fellowship
of Reformational Churches

Contents

Section	Questions
The Cost	1-5
The Deity and Creation	6-10
Glory	11-15
Trinity and Incarnation	16-20
Man's Essence and Purpose	21-25
Male and Female	26-30
Original Sin	31-35
Revelation	36-40
Covenant of Life	41-45
The Fall of Man	46-50
Consequences of Sin	51-55
Deliverance	56-60
Christ as the New Adam	61-65
Covenant of Grace	66-70
Mosaic Covenant	71-75
Covenant Law	76-80
The Ten Commandments: Laws of Worship	81-85
The Ten Commandments: The Sabbath Day	86-90
The Ten Commandments: Human Relationships	91-95
The Commandment to Love	96-100
Old Covenant Signs	101-105
The Law of the Spirit of Life	106-110
Predestination	111-115
Repentance	116-120
Justification	121-125
Adoption and Sanctification	126-130
The Means of Grace	131-135
Sacraments	136-140
Baptism	141-145
Efficacy of Baptism	146-150
The Lord's Supper	151-155
Efficacy of the Lord's Supper	156-160
Prayer	161-165
Model of Prayer	166-170
Saving Faith	171-175
Assurance	176-180

Contents continued

Section	Questions
Hope	181-185
Fruits of the Spirit	186-190
Virtue	191-195
Humility	196-200
Perseverance	201-205
Nature of Salvation	206-210
Sphere Authority	211-215
Nature of the Church	216-220
The Church Organic	221-225
Church Government	226-230
Authority of Overseers	231-235
The Purpose of the Church	236-240
Offices of Christ	241-245
Functions of the State	246-250
The Forces of Darkness	251-255
Judgment	256-260

"...and we rejoice in the hope of the glory of God. Not only that, but we rejoice in our sufferings..."

Romans 5:2

Preface

Why another reformed catechism?

Many reformation-based catechisms have been composed and disseminated in the church throughout the centuries, but the three most significant and widely used in the Reformed and Presbyterian churches have been the Heidelberg and the Westminster Shorter and Larger. Yet these were produced hundreds of years ago. This is not to say that these tools have fallen out of favor or become obsolete – to the contrary. They are very much as significant now as ever. But they don't speak to every point of doctrine, and frankly, they tend to be a little weak in the area of sanctification, the doctrine of how the Christian faith is played out upon the stage.

You will find within these pages an emphasis on the content of faith and the means of grace, particularly the way in which the concepts of glory, hope, and suffering interact for the Christian in our daily pursuit of holiness. There is a strong emphasis on the role of sacraments in this pursuit, on man's purpose in dominion, on the battle against the kingdom of darkness, and on the need for loyalty to Christ in relation to the grace of assurance.

This is meant to be a tool. Having two hundred sixty questions and fifty-two sections, it is designed to be broken up into five questions a week for a year. It might be used in family devotions, or teaching lessons, or even Lord's Day liturgy. It is meant to be personalized and is accompanied by further questions for the purpose of stirring up self-examination.

This catechism is in no way meant to replace the Heidelberg or the Westminster, but is merely an attempt to compliment those great resources with a vision for the church moving forward, keeping always reformation in mind where it is needed.

~ 2024

The Cost

Q1 – What must you do to be saved?

A – I must deny myself, take up my cross daily, and follow Jesus.

Matthew 16:24-26, 10:38-39...Mark 9:34-38...Romans 12:1

Q2 – What does it mean to deny yourself?

A – It means to die to myself, putting to death my own appetites, urges, and earthly desires in favor of God's glory.

Mark 9:38...1 Peter 1:10-11

Q3 – What is symbolized by the cross?

A – Suffering, affliction, curses, and death.

Matthew 27: 32-35...Hebrews 12:2...Galatians 3:13

Q4 – Must you suffer daily in order to be saved?

A – I must be willing to deny myself every day for the sake of Jesus, but it is only through his own suffering that my self-denial is justified and able to save me.

Philippians 1:29...Romans 8:16-17...1 Corinthians 15:31

Q5 – How does Jesus' suffering become your suffering?

A – Only through faith in him.

Philippians 3:7-11...2 Corinthians 5:14-15...Romans 5:1-3

Questions for Self-Examination and Prayer

What aspects of my life have become a hindrance to my following Jesus? Am I willing to part with those things that have become a hindrance to me?

How much suffering am I willing to endure for the sake of following Christ?

How might my suffering glorify God? Can God's glory shine in every instance of my suffering?

Most gracious God of your suffering servant, grant me the wisdom and strength to deny myself those things that keep me from Christ, and may his affliction be for me the path that I would follow unto everlasting life.

The Deity and Creation

Q6 – Who is Jesus?
A – The man Jesus is the Christ my savior, the Lord God incarnate, the only begotten Son of the Most High God.
John 3:16...John 4:42...1 Timothy 4:10

Q7 – Who is the Most High God?
A – The Lord is the Most High God. He is the Creator of the heavens and the earth, the God of Abraham, Isaac, and Jacob.
Psalms 47, 124:8...Genesis 1:1...Isaiah 42:8...Isaiah 45...Exodus 3:6, 14-15

Q8 – How did the Most High God create the heavens and the earth?
A – God created the heavens and the earth out of nothing, by the Word of his power, and effectually good.
Colossians 1:15-16...Ephesians 3:9...Psalms 33:6...Jeremiah 32:17...John 1:1-4

Q9 – Of what does heaven and earth consist?
A – Heaven and earth consists of all things both visible and invisible, both supernatural and natural, being distinct from God in substance, yet dependent upon God for existence.
Colossians 1:16...1 Corinthians 8:6...Revelation 4:11

Q10 – What is the Most High God like?
A – God is magnificent in glory, immortal, good, faithful, just, holy and wise, compassionate and gracious, slow to anger and abounding in steadfast love.
1 Chronicles 29:10-13...1 Timothy 1:17...Psalms 9, 103:8-9, 145:8-9...Romans 4:8...Isaiah 42:3...Jeremiah 9:24

Questions for Self-Examination and Prayer

Do I ever consider the significance of the Creator of the world becoming part of his own creation?

Why would a God so high and mighty care for a creature as lowly as myself?

In what ways do I tend to forget my dependence upon God as his creature?

Almighty Lord of all creation, you alone are the Most High God. Open my eyes to see your magnificence. May I meditate upon your perfect attributes that I might know you as you would have me know you, even in your incarnate Son.

Glory

Q11 – What is glory?
A – Glory is the joy of God, the brilliance of his excellence displayed in beauty and strength.

Ezekiel 10:4, 1:27-28...Exodus 24:17, 33:28-33...Psalms 147:10-11...Nehemiah 8:7-11

Q12 – Does glory rightly belong to any of God's creatures?
A – Glory belongs to God alone, but he is graciously pleased to share his glory with his creatures, especially mankind.

Psalms 8:5, 19:1, 71:8...Romans 9:23...1 Corinthians 3:18

Q13 – Is mankind able to abuse the glory that belongs exclusively to the Most High God?
A – Yes. Mankind can abuse God's glory by failing to recognize it, by stealing it for himself, or by attempting to discredit his excellent reputation.

Romans 1:22-23, 3:23

Q14 – Why should God's glory be recognized by mankind?
A – The recognition of God's glory is necessary for virtuous living and for exercising dominion within the created order.

Psalms 29...1 Corinthians 10:31...Jeremiah 9:23-24...Romans 5:1-4

Q15 – How can your self-denial bring joy to God and magnify his excellence?
A – Because God's beauty and strength are perfected in my weakness, and my life rests in this hope.

Romans 5:1-4...2 Corinthians 12:9-10...1 Corinthians 15:36, 42-43...Ecclesiastes 3:11

Questions for Self-Examination and Prayer

In what ways do I fail to see God's glory in my everyday life? Is his glory evident in the mundane?

How have I attempted to rob God of his glory? In what ways do I tend to discredit his reputation, even unintentionally?

How does the knowledge of God's glory affect my decision making? How should it affect my relationships with others?

Glorious Lord, may the glory of your presence not be lost upon me, for you alone are worthy of all glory, honor, and praise because your power is made perfect in my weakness and your help is the strength of my weary soul.

Trinity and Incarnation

Q16 – What is God?
A – God is immaterial spirit, being one substantive deity in three distinct persons, having unity and equality in essence and purpose.
Deuteronomy 6:4...Luke 3:21-22...1 Peter 1:1-2...Isaiah 44:3,6

Q17 – Who are the three distinct persons existing as one deity?
A – God the Father, God the Son, and God the Holy Spirit.
John 17:1-5, 15:26...Matthew 28:19, 3:16-17...1 Peter 1:1-2...2 Corinthians 13:13

Q18 – If Jesus is God the Son, then how can he be man as well?
A – The Son of God was incarnated in the womb of the virgin Mary, conceived supernaturally by the power of the Holy Spirit apart from the seed of man, yet grew inside her naturally until birth.
Luke 1:26-33, 2:4-7...Matthew 1:22-23

Q19 – In what consists the glory of the incarnation?
A – God the Son, by virtue of his incarnation, took to himself true humanity and is consequently fully God and fully man, two distinct natures in one person forever.
Psalms 8...Hebrews 1:2-3, 2:14...John 1:14

Q20 – Why was God the Son willing to become man?
A – Because Jesus, as the Christ of God, needed to become man in order to experience the suffering of man.
Hebrews 1:3, 2:17...Philippians 2:5-8

Questions for Self-Examination and Prayer

Why is it crucial to have a correct view of the Trinity? How might it affect other doctrines and the way I live?

How tolerant should I be with others who may have an incorrect or confused understanding of the Trinity?

Do I have difficulty accepting doctrines that my mind cannot explain? How should I respond?

Lord, teach me the glory of your Godhead and to submit to the mysteries of your eternity. Your ways are beyond my full comprehension. Humble me in the knowledge of the Holy.

Man's Essence and Purpose

Q21 – Why would God the Son be willing to experience the suffering of man?
A – Because only through suffering unto death could the curse of death upon man be broken in order that man may live through the suffering that leads to glory.
John 3:16...Hebrews 12:2...Galatians 3:13-14...Philippians 3:9-11

Q22 – Why could not another man have broken the curse?
A – Because only a perfect man, not by nature liable to the curse, but who is also by nature the essence and substance of God, would be qualified to break the curse by virtue of experiencing the curse.
1 Peter 1:18-20...Leviticus 6:5-7...Matthew 1:20-22

Q23 – What is man?
A – Man is the image of God in flesh, yet inferior, subordinate, and mortal.
Psalms 144:3-4...Genesis 1:27...Genesis 6:3

Q24 – How can man, who is body and flesh, reflect the image of God who is immaterial?
A – Man is not flesh only but is a union of body and spirit called a living soul.
Genesis 2:7...1 Thessalonians 5:23...Revelation 20:4...Hebrews 4:12...1 Corinthians 15:45

Q25 – Is man's spiritual nature the only way in which he bears God's image?
A – No. God created man to bear the image of his glory, exercising dominion over the earth as prophet, priest, and king.
Genesis 1:28...Jeremiah 9:23-24...1 Corinthians 11:7...1 Peter 2:5...Hebrews 2:6-8

Questions for Self-Examination and Prayer

What is significant in the paradox that life may only be found through death? Am I willing to go down that road?

Do I treat others as if they are image bearers of God? Do I treat myself that way?

What would my life look like if I took dominion seriously?

Sovereign Lord, I don't know why you have chosen to create me in this state of privilege, but forgive me for not using your image as is proper. May every corner of my life be lived in submission to your Lordship.

Male and Female

Q26 – How, then, was man originally created?

A – Man was created male and female, formed from the dust of the earth and given life by God's own breath.

Genesis 1:27...Genesis 2:7

Q27 – Does woman also keep dominion after God's image?

A – Woman was formed from the body and substance of man, not independent, but dependent. That is why we can say that God made man male and female, after his own image, with dominion over the earthly creatures.

1 Corinthians 11:7-9, 11-12...Genesis 2:21-22

Q28 – Why does man need woman?

A – As a helpmate in dominion, to honor him, to serve him, to challenge him, and to bear offspring for his name's sake.

Genesis 2:18, 24...Ephesians 5:25-33

Q29 – Why does woman need man?

A – As a headship, to lead her, to love her, to protect her, to provide for her, and to name her.

1 Corinthians 11:3...Genesis 2:23, 3:20...Ephesians 5:22-24

Q30 – How is the relationship between man and woman kept most honorable?

A – Through a faithful, enduring marriage union and the preservation of family, that being the supreme institution established among men.

Exodus 20:14...Hebrews 13:4-5...1 Corinthians 7:1-5...2 Corinthians 6:14-15...Mark 10:11-12

Questions for Self-Examination and Prayer

How influenced am I by feminism, the doctrine that a woman's identity exists apart from man?

In what ways can a man love and care for his wife without emasculating himself?

In what ways can I better keep my marriage honorable? Of what do I need to repent?

Good Father, help me to submit to your authority, even in your created order and purpose for male and female. Give me the strength and boldness to stand firm for what is right and repudiate the lies of the current age.

Original Sin

Q31 – From what, then, do you need to be saved?
A – From sin, death, and hell.

James 1:15...Revelation 20:14-15...Romans 5:8-10, 7:24...1 John 3:4...Luke 12:5

Q32 – What is sin?
A – Sin is rebellion against God's authority.

James 4:17...Romans 3:9-12...1 John 3:4...1 Corinthians 6:9-11

Q33 – How is sin manifest?
A – Sin is manifest in thought, word, and deed, and also in fallen nature.

Genesis 4:6-8...Romans 7:14-20...Ephesians 5:3-7

Q34 – What is fallen nature?
A – Fallen nature is the rebellious nature of the whole man.

Psalms 51:5, 53:2-3...Ephesians 2:1-3...Romans 7:5, 17-18

Q35 – From where is fallen nature derived?
A – Adam's sin corrupted not only his own nature, but also that of his posterity, being that his guilt was imputed unto and his rebellion inherited by all those naturally conceived, leading to actual transgressions against God's revealed will.

Romans 3:23, 5:12-14, 7:19-20...Colossians 2:13...Psalms 51:3-5

Questions for Self-Examination and Prayer

What good have I ever done that sin has not been a part of it as well?

May I use ignorance as an excuse for my sin?

What particular sins assault me to the point of failing to recognize other sins?

In what ways is it a good thing to know that sin is always before me?

Gracious Father, save me from my lawlessness and rebellion which lead to destruction. My thoughts, words, and actions have been an offense to your holy nature, and I need your righteous mercy.

Revelation

Q36 – What is God's revealed will?
A – God's revealed will is his law.
Deuteronomy 6:6-7, 12:28, 29:29...Exodus 24:1-5

Q37 – How has God's law been revealed to you?
A – By the testimony of his eternal Word entrusted to his prophets and apostles and recorded in human language.
Hebrews 1:1...1 Peter 1:10-11...1Thessalonians 2:13

Q38 – Where is the eternal Word to be found?
A – In the sacred, infallible scriptures of the Old and New Testaments and in the person of Christ Jesus.
Hebrews 1:2...Matthew 5:17-18...2 Timothy 3:15-17

Q39 – How does Christ Jesus personify the eternal Word of God found in the sacred scriptures?
A – Being that Christ is the eternal Word of God incarnate, and being that the sacred scriptures are the divinely inspired testimony of Christ Jesus, we may rightly regard the sacred scriptures as the eternal Word of God.
John 1:14, 6:68...Luke 24:27

Q40 – What is the primary narrative of the sacred scriptures?
A – The scriptures reveal the Christ in the history of creation, rebellion, and redemption specific to the covenants God has made with his church, for the glory of God alone in Christ.
Psalms 78...Psalms 106...Matthew 26:52-56...Luke 24:25-27...1 Corinthians 15:1-8

Questions for Self-Examination and Prayer

Do I seek God's revealed will as I ought? Do I go to the council of his Word for my decisions?

How can I better honor God's sacred scriptures in my life?

When I read God's Word, do I see Christ revealed to me?

Eternal God, reveal yourself to me in your Word. Open my eyes to see Christ in all of scripture that I might know your law and believe the good news of him who saves me.

Covenant of Life

Q41 – How was God's law first given and prescribed?

A – God's law was first given in the form of a covenant and prescribed to Adam when he was created.
Genesis 2:15-17

Q42 – What were the stipulations of God's covenant with Adam?

A – God gave life to Adam at his creation, but if he was to transgress the law instituted by God for the governing of his life, then he would die in body and soul.
Genesis 2:17

Q43 – What was the law that God instituted for Adam's governance?

A – God commanded man to be fruitful and to fill the earth and subdue it while forbidding him to eat fruit from the tree of the knowledge of good and evil.
Genesis 2:17...Genesis 3:17

Q44 – What is death?

A – Death is the destruction of body and soul as the consequence of rebellion against God.
Genesis 3:19...Romans 5:12

Q45 – What is hell?

A – Hell is the eternal destination of all mankind who die apart from Christ where God's just wrath is poured out upon them in torment forever.
Revelation 20:13-15...Matthew 13:41-43...Mark 9:43-48

Questions for Self-Examination and Prayer

What is the contrast between subduing the earth and eating the fruit of the knowledge of good and evil?

How might God use my choices in his greater plan for humanity?

Do I take the time to think about sin, death, and hell? Or do I avoid thinking about it?

Heavenly Father, I entrust my destiny into your gracious hands. Let me not be discouraged by what I don't understand, but rather let me take comfort knowing that you are a God of covenant, a God of promise and fulfillment.

The Fall of Man

Q46 – Did God create the first man, Adam, to sin?
A – God created Adam with the ability to sin, but also upright so that he had not the inclination to sin.
Genesis 1:31...Ecclesiastes 7:29

Q47 – In what manner did Adam first sin?
A – Adam first sinned by eating the forbidden fruit, thereby breaking God's covenant law.
Genesis 3:6-7

Q48 – Why then, did Adam sin if he had no inclination?
A – Adam's motivation is a mystery that has not been revealed to mankind, but it is evident that he chose to sin only after his wife, Eve, first sinned in her own person by eating the forbidden fruit.
Genesis 3:1,6

Q49 – Why did Eve first sin?
A – Eve first sinned because the serpent deceived her into thinking that eating the forbidden fruit would reap blessings instead of curses.
Genesis 3:6...1 Timothy 2:14

Q50 – Who is the serpent?
A – The serpent is a devil, a rebellious creature of spiritual origin, a deceiver and conniving usurper of the dominion granted to man at creation.
Genesis 3:13-15...Revelation 12:9...2 Corinthians 11:3

Questions for Self-Examination and Prayer

How does sin tend to overtake me in my life, even when I am not expecting it?

What activities can I avoid to protect me against temptation?

What is my first inclination when tempted? Do I turn to God's Word? Do I tend to pray? Or do I push my conscience aside because it interferes with my desires?

Most compassionate Father, give me grace moment by moment that I might make godly decisions when tempted. Let not my desires overtake me, but come to my aid that I might know you as my deliverer and delight myself in what is right and good.

Consequences of Sin

Q51 – What was the consequence of sinning by eating the forbidden fruit?
A – Man, who was created upright, fell into sin and misery, bringing the curse of death upon himself and his posterity.
Ephesians 2:1...Genesis 2:17, 3:17-18...Deuteronomy 5:9

Q52 – Why was all mankind thereafter cursed for the sin of the first man?
A – Because God created Adam to be the federal head of his posterity; the prophet, priest, and king over all the earth.
1 Corinthians 11:7-9...Genesis 1:27-28, 2:7-8,15

Q53 – What is a federal head?
A – One who represents me in covenant, whereby his actions are accounted to my own behalf.
Job 1:4-5...Ephesians 5:23...2 Samuel 24:10-17...Romans 5:18-19

Q54 – How is sin and misery manifest as a consequence of Adam's first sin?
A – As Adam's offspring, I fall short of the glory of God and am by nature dead in sin, alienated from God, subject to his wrath and curse, liable to every kind of affliction, unable to attain to any spiritual good or understanding, utterly corrupted in my entire being, and without godly affection or purpose.
Romans 3:10-18, 8:7-8...Ephesians 2:3

Q55 – Why does God hold you guilty for the sins of a representative?
A – Because there is no point in my life that I am not a willing participant in Adam's transgression. But even more so, if I am not condemned through a representative, it would make little sense that I could be delivered through one.
Romans 5:12-19

Questions for Self-Examination and Prayer

Think about federal headship. Is it not an integral part of the created order? What aspects of life is this most prevalent?

Am I better than Adam? Would I have succeeded when confronted with his dilemma?

How does the sin and misery of my fallen nature show itself in my day to day tendencies?

Lord, my sins overwhelm me. My condemnation is just. I cannot stand on my own. Save me.

Deliverance

Q56 – What is the faith by which Jesus' suffering becomes your suffering and delivers you from the curse of death?

A – Saving faith.

Galatians 3:13-14...Ephesians 2:8...Acts 26:18...1 Peter 1:5...Philippians 3:8-10

Q57 – Of what does saving faith consist?

A – Saving faith consists of believing that Jesus is the Christ and coming to him for rest, trusting in his desire and power to save me, and pledging my allegiance to him above all else.

John 20:31...Matthew 10:38-39, 11:28-30...Galatians 2:20

Q58 – On what basis may you find rest in Christ Jesus?

A – Jesus was able to satisfy God's justice by offering himself in body and soul as a sacrifice for my sin, turning God's wrath away from me by taking it upon himself.

Romans 3:24-25...1 Peter 3:18...Matthew 26:38-39

Q59 – How was Jesus qualified to atone for your sin?

A – Because, like Adam, he is my federal head; but unlike Adam, he knew no sin because, though tempted, he kept God's law perfectly.

Hebrews 2:6-9...1 Peter 2:22...2 Corinthians 5:21...Romans 5:19...John 8:46...Isaiah 53

Q60 – How can one innocent man's sacrifice on behalf of a guilty man be considered just?

A – Because Christ's atonement was a willing sacrifice and one of infinite worth.

Romans 5:6-10...Matthew 5:17-18...Philippians 2:5-8...John 10:17-18

Questions for Self-Examination and Prayer

How closely is faith associated with suffering in my own life?

Do I tend to live as if Jesus' suffering is meant to pave the way for affluence in my life?

Do I really live as if Jesus has the power and desire to save me? Or do I trust in my own abilities?

Kind Lord, sometimes this life is too overwhelming. Forgive me for not living out what I claim to believe. Who can deliver me from this body of death? Thanks be to Christ.

Christ as the New Adam

Q61 – In what way was Jesus tempted to sin?
A – Jesus was tempted in every way that I am, yet without sin.
Hebrews 2:18, 4:15...Mark 1:13

Q62 – What law did Jesus keep perfectly?
A – Since Jesus maintained his upright nature throughout his life despite every temptation, he conformed himself perfectly to the covenant of life that Adam failed to keep.
1 John 3:5...John 17:6-8...Romans 5:19

Q63 – Was Jesus, being the Son of God, able to sin?
A – Yes, otherwise his temptations would not have been true temptations, but at no time did he sin.
Hebrews 4:15

Q64 – Where were Christ's temptations most acute?
A – In the wilderness, weak from hunger, confronted by the devil himself, and also in the garden, weak from passion, confronted by mortality.
Matthew 4:1-11, 26:36-46...Luke 4:1-3...Luke 22:39-45

Q65 – Was the law of the covenant of life the only law that Jesus was required to keep?
A – Jesus also perfectly kept the law of Moses which God prescribed to the children of Israel in the form of a covenant now referred to as the old covenant.
Luke 2:21-27...Galatians 4:4-5...Matthew 5:17, 15:1-6...John 8:46

Questions for Self-Examination and Prayer

Is suffering merely a result of sin? Or is it natural for imperfect humanity?

Is temptation a form of suffering?

Knowing that Christ was tempted just as I am, what should my response be?

Lord, help me understand the power of Christ over my temptations in this life, and may I never cease to remember with gladness his active obedience to your law on my behalf.

Covenant of Grace

Q66 – Why did God make a covenant with the children of Israel?

A – Because as mankind lost communion with God by breaking the covenant made in Adam, God still desired a people to be holy unto himself, to bear the glory of his image, and to govern the earth as prophets, priests, and kings.

Genesis 12:1-3...2 Corinthians 6:16-18...Isaiah 61:1-7...Exodus 6:2-8, 19:6

Q67 – Of what does the covenant with Israel consist?

A – It consists of God's grace and redemption.

Deuteronomy 7:6-8...Romans 3:23-24...Exodus 20:1-2

Q68 – With whom was the covenant of grace made?

A – It was made with Abraham, the patriarch of Israel, whom God promised would become the father of the faithful throughout the whole earth.

Genesis 3:14-15, 17:1-8...Exodus 2:23-25

Q69 – What promises did God give to Abraham?

A – God promised to be Abraham's God, to bless his Seed (which is the Christ), and to give his descendants the land occupied by the Canaanites.

Genesis 15:5, 17:7-8...Galatians 3:16-18,29...Romans 4:16, 9:6-8...Hebrews 11:17-18

Q70 – What were the stipulations of this covenant of grace that God made with Abraham?

A – God required faith in his promises of redemption through use of his covenant signs.

Genesis 15:4-6, 17:9-10...Romans 4:13, 6:3-4

Questions for Self-Examination and Prayer

What is my purpose upon this earth?

How can I better serve God as a prophet, priest, and king over his creation?

How does being in covenant with God affect the way I view myself?

Covenant God, give me the faith to use my time and energy for your purpose, not mine.

Mosaic Covenant

Q71 – When did these blessings come to pass?
A – When God delivered the children of Israel out of their bondage in Egypt, he inaugurated the promised blessings through his prophet Moses by way of a national covenant with the children of Israel.
Exodus 6:1-8, 13:3, 20:2

Q72 – Of what aspects did this national covenant exist?
A – There are two aspects of God's national covenant with Israel through Moses: a temporal and a spiritual.
Exodus 6:6-7...Romans 9:6-8

Q73 – What is the temporal aspect of the Mosaic covenant with Israel?
A – It is like the covenant of life God made with Adam. If Israel would keep God's laws faithfully, he would bless them, protect them, and prosper them. However, if they would turn away and follow other gods, then God would cut them off as a covenant nation.
Deuteronomy 28

Q74 – Did Israel keep covenant with God as a nation?
A – No. The children of Israel fell into willful idolatry time and time again, forgetting God's mercies and invoking his wrath against them.
Matthew 21:18-19, 33-45, 23:37-39

Q75 – What is the spiritual aspect of the Mosaic covenant with Israel?
A – The covenant was not national only, but a picture of a redeemed humanity that God is creating from the ashes of fallen mankind.
Genesis 17:4...Isaiah 49:6...Romans 11:25-27

Questions for Self-Examination and Prayer

In what ways am I similar to the children of Israel? What idolatry do I commit? What mercies do I forget?

In what ways does the modern church mirror the children of Israel?

Lord, have mercy upon me, a sinner. Let me be a part of the redeemed humanity that you are creating. May you save your church from the corruption of this wicked generation, for the sake of Christ and covenant.

Covenant Law

Q76 – How did God assure his faithful people regarding this covenant of grace?
A – Through laws, signs, rituals, and feasts.
Deuteronomy 6:1-9...Exodus 12:14...Romans 9:3-5

Q77 – What laws were instituted to assure God's people of his gracious covenant?
A – Three types of laws were instituted: moral laws, ceremonial laws, and civil laws.
Deuteronomy 5:1-22...Leviticus 26:46

Q78 – What is the essence of moral laws?
A – Moral laws reflect God's holy character, mirror the law written on the conscience of mankind, and are perpetually binding, establishing a standard of righteous conduct.
Exodus 20:1-17...Leviticus 11:45...2 Peter 1:5-11...Matthew 19:16-27...James 2:8-11

Q79 – What is the essence of ceremonial laws?
A – Ceremonial laws reminded the people of God's holiness and their own need for cleansing, foreshadowing the coming of the Christ and being eventually fulfilled during his earthly ministry by the new covenant established in his blood.
Leviticus 1:1-9...Hebrews 7:11-13, 9:23-28...Galatians 3:19-25...Romans 3:20

Q80 – What is the essence of civil laws?
A – Civil laws were given to govern the commonwealth of Israel according to God's standards of justice.
Deuteronomy 10:17-19, 16:18-20...Matthew 18:21-35, 23:23...Philippians 4:8

Questions for Self-Examination and Prayer

Is God's law a delight to me? What are some things that I value more than God's law?

What does justice look like? Where does it come from?

How can I get in the habit of thinking God's thoughts after him?

Almighty God, teach me to delight in your law. May it be sweet to my senses and a lamp unto my feet. May it drive me to the arms of my Savior.

The Ten Commandments: Laws of Worship

Q81 – Where is the law primarily found?
A – The law is expounded in the writings of Moses but is most pointedly summarized in the Ten Commandments and the law of love.
Exodus 20:1-19...Deuteronomy 5:6-21, 6:4-6...Matthew 5:43-48, 22:37-40

Q82 – What are the Ten Commandments?
A – The Ten Commandments are the laws which God spoke from the mountain, wrote with his own hand on tablets of stone, and delivered to his people as their obligation of allegiance.
Exodus 20:1-19, 32:18, 34:2

Q83 – What is the content of the Ten Commandments?
A – The Ten Commandments are given in three distinct parts.

Q84 – What is the first part of the Ten Commandments?
A – My duty to God, namely that in my thoughts, words, and actions, I must show allegiance to no god except the Lord, I must not worship him by the use of any vain or forbidden practice, and that I must not bear or use his name in any vain, empty, or profane way.
Exodus 20:2-7...Deuteronomy 5:7-11

Q85 – Are these first three commandments still binding to this day?
A – Yes. Being that God is the sovereign Creator, he alone is qualified to determine what acts, modes, and forms of worship he will accept from his creatures.
Deuteronomy 12:31-32...Acts 17:23-25...Ezekiel 1:28...Psalms 29:1-2, 96:8-9...Exodus 20:2...Leviticus 11:44, 18:21, 19:4...2 Samuel 6:6-8

Questions for Self-Examination and Prayer

Does God care about the way I worship him? If so, am I worshiping him in his prescribed way?

How do I respect God's holiness when I worship?

What does true worship entail? Do the things I say in my day-to-day business matter to God?

Does God really care what I do as long as my heart is sincere?

God of law and grace, forgive me of the idolatry in my heart and for withholding from you the glory you deserve. Set your servant apart that I might worship you only.

The Ten Commandments: The Sabbath Day

Q86 – What is the second part of the Ten Commandments?
A – That I must remember the Sabbath day to keep it holy.
Exodus 20:8-11...Deuteronomy 5:12-15

Q87 – What is the Sabbath day?
A – It is the day of rest for the people of God prescribed to be kept on the seventh day of the week.
Exodus 16:29-30, 20:8-10, 23:20-13

Q88 – Why did God require a day of rest each week for his people?
A – So that they would remember God's grace and salvation and find their rest from the yoke of the law in God alone.
Mark 2:27-28...Exodus 31:12-17...Isaiah 58:13-14...Acts 15:10-11

Q89 – Is this fourth commandment still binding to this day?
A – No. This commandment, being ceremonial in nature and specific to the children of Israel under the old covenant, is no longer to be kept on the seventh day.
Colossians 2:16-17...Acts 18:4-6

Q90 – Is there then no longer any requirement to keep the Sabbath day holy?
A – Since Christ Jesus is the fulfillment of the rest promised by God for his people, the Sabbath day is kept by faith in Christ apart from the works of the law, resting in Christ alone for salvation.
John 5:16-18...Hebrews 4:1-3, 7-11...Matthew 11:28-30

Questions for Self-Examination and Prayer

When life is hectic and troubling, am I finding rest in Christ? Or am I looking elsewhere?

What is the connection between holiness and the Sabbath?

As I rest in Christ, do I find myself concerned with being holy?

How do I view time and days? Am I giving my time to Christ or taking it for myself?

Sabbath Lord, what would my life look like if I gave all my time to you? May you give me the rest that only Christ can provide.

The Ten Commandments: Human Relationships

Q91 – What is the third part of the Ten Commandments?
A – My duty to man, namely that I must honor my father and mother, that I do not murder others, that I do not commit adultery, that I do not steal, that I do not bear false witness against others, and that I do not covet anything that belongs to my neighbor.
Exodus 20:12-17...Deuteronomy5:16-21

Q92 – How is your duty to man to be applied?
A – By internal conformity to the law in thoughts and attitudes as well as external conformity in words and deeds.
Matthew 5:21-22, 12:34-35, 15:11...1 Samuel 15:22

Q93 – In what ways are you required to conform internally to the laws concerning your duty to man?
A – By respecting authority, especially that of my parents, by not hating others, by not lusting after immorality, by not envying others, by not harboring deceit, and by being content.
Matthew 5:22-28...1 John 2:15-17...1 Corinthians 13:4-7

Q94 – In what way are you required to conform externally to the laws concerning your duty to man?
A – By avoiding the things I am forbidden to do and by doing that which I am commanded to do.
Romans 1:28-31...Galatians 5:19-21...Revelation 21:8

Q95 – Are these six commandments still binding today?
A – Yes. They are reflections of the moral character of God and therefore requirements for his covenant people to live holy lives.
1 Peter 1:15-16...Romans 2:26-27, 7:12...1 John 3:7

Questions for Self-Examination and Prayer

Do I really notice my sins day to day? Or do I only notice the big ones? How can I better know myself?

Am I the type of person who thinks outward conformity is enough? Or sincerity is enough?

Consider the variety of ways I might break God's law. How can I ever claim to be without fault?

Heavenly Father, show me my sins and let me despise myself. I mistreat my neighbor every day and harbor enmity in my heart. I thank you for Jesus who kept your law always. May I desire to treat my neighbor as I would be treated, with mercy and kindness.

The Commandment to Love

Q96 – What is the law of love?
A – That I must love God with all my heart, mind, soul, and strength, and that I must love my neighbor as myself.
Galatians 5:14...Deuteronomy 6:4...Matthew 22:36-39

Q97 – What does loving God look like?
A – My love for God is not merely affection for him, but it is also obedience to him.
John 14:15, 23-24...1 John 2:4-6...2 John 2:6

Q98 – What does loving your neighbor look like?
A – Love for my neighbor is not necessarily affection for him, but it is self-sacrifice for his good and doing justice on his behalf.
1 John 4:7-11...Romans 13:9-10...1 Corinthians 13:4-7...Matthew 7:12

Q99 – Is the law of love greater than the Ten Commandments?
A – It is neither greater nor lesser. The Ten Commandments are merely particular ways in which loving God and my neighbor are manifest.
2 John 1:5...Matthew 5:43-44...Joshua 22:5

Q100 – Are the Ten Commandments merely examples, then?
A – No. They are laws by which I commit treason if I break any one of them in thought, word, or deed.
Exodus 20:4-6...Amos 2:4...Deuteronomy 28:15...James 2:8-10

Questions for Self-Examination and Prayer

Can I love God without loving his law?

How seriously is God concerned about my smaller sins? Is there any sin that does not condemn?

Am I capable of loving God and my neighbor the way that God requires? Do I love God as I ought?

What does it mean to do justice on behalf of my neighbor? Might doing justice sometimes appear harsh to my neighbor? If so, what might this look like?

Lord, open my eyes that I might see your love in your law. Teach me to put my neighbor's needs before mine, and let me learn to show kindness even to those who despise me.

Old Covenant Signs

Q101 – What signs were instituted to assure God's people of his gracious covenant?
A – Many signs were given, but the two most prominent were circumcision and the passover meal.
Genesis 17:1-14...Exodus 12

Q102 – What did circumcision signify?
A – It signified the cutting of covenant between God and his people, the need for bloodshed to gain right standing before God, and a mark validating God's promises to Abraham.
Colossians 2:11...Genesis 17:14

Q103 – What did the passover meal signify?
A – It signified the occasion when God delivered his people from bondage through vindication and bloodshed.
Exodus 12:12-14

Q104 – Is circumcision and the passover meal still required for your observance today?
A – No, because old covenant ordinances only foreshadowed Christ, but Christ has since established a new covenant in his own blood.
Colossians 2:11-13...Galatians 6:15...Romans 4:9-11...1 Corinthians 5:6-8

Q105 – Does the Mosaic law, then, have no power to redeem you from sin?
A – Since due to my fallen nature I am dead to God, the Mosaic law has no power to redeem because it only makes my sin all the more sinful.
Romans 3:19-20, 28, 7:10-13...Galatians 3:19

Questions for Self-Examination and Prayer

Why must God's grace require such violence?

How can sin become even more sinful? What does the law reveal about me?

What comfort can I derive from knowing that God is a covenant God?

Gracious Father, I confess that my life is messy and my sins abundant, but I know also that your grace is greater than all of my sins and that you will use even the messiness for your righteous ends.

The Law of the Spirit of Life

Q106 – Is there any law, then, that has the power to redeem you from sin?

A – Only the law of the Spirit of life has the power to redeem me from the law of sin and death.

Romans 8:2...Galatians 5:1-6...Ephesians 2:11-13

Q107 – Is the law of the Spirit of life at odds with the written, revealed law?

A – On the contrary, the law of the Spirit of life is the grace of God in which the written, revealed law is fulfilled in Christ.

Romans 3:30-31, 8:1-4, 10:4

Q108 – Where is the law of the Spirit of life to be found?

A – The law of the Spirit of life is found only by faith in Christ Jesus who put my sin to death by becoming death for me in order that the righteousness of the law might be fully met in me.

Romans 3:21-22,25, 8:3-4

Q109 – On what grounds can you trust and be assured of God's desire to save you if you are dead in your fallen nature?

A – On the grounds of God's promise of redemption in Christ Jesus.

1 Timothy 2:3-4...1 Corinthians 1:30...1 Peter 3:18

Q110 – How does God make it possible for fallen man, dead in sin, to trust in him?

A – Because he who created me has also the power to redeem me and grant new life to me.

Matthew 19:25-26...Ephesians 2:4-6,8-9...2 Corinthians 5:17

Questions for Self-Examination and Prayer

In what ways has the law of sin and death had mastery over me?

Have I learned to recognize the law of the Spirit of life? Can I think of examples of God's grace in my life?

What does it mean that the righteousness of the law is fully met in me?

When do I find it most difficult to believe that God has the power to redeem me from my sins?

Sovereign Lord, awaken a sense of your grace in my soul and bind me to the One who is my righteousness. May your Spirit of Life do a good work in my heart that I might be recognized as yours.

Predestination

Q111 – How does God manifest and exercise this power to redeem?

A – God has determined whom he will redeem, in accordance with the counsel of his own will, from eternity past.

Ephesians 1:3-6,11...Romans 8:30...2 Timothy 1:9

Q112 – Has God determined that all mankind will be redeemed?

A – No, only those who will trust him.

Romans 9:19-21...Luke 13:23-24...John 1:12, 3:16...Ephesians 1:11-12

Q113 – What else has God determined from eternity past?

A – From eternity past, God has foreordained whatsoever comes to pass.

Acts 2:23...Proverbs 16:4, 19:21...Job 42:2...Deuteronomy 32:39...Lamentations 3:37-38

Q114 – Is man, then, bound by fate?

A – No. God ordains the means as well as the ends, a contingency of secondary causes, so that the freedom of man and nature are established by God's will rather than restricted by it.

Proverbs 6:33...Deuteronomy 29:29...Genesis 50:20...Philippians 1:12

Q115 – But, though foreordained unto redemption, how will you then trust God if you are dead in sin?

A – The Holy Spirit imparts faith to me so that I will trust Christ for salvation.

1 John 5:4...Ephesians 2:1,8...Romans 8:11

Questions for Self-Examination and Prayer

How does a contingency of secondary causes explain the problem of evil?

If God did not determine whatsoever comes to pass, could I really trust him with my own destiny?

What does it mean to say that God is sovereign? Do I tend to make decisions by chance, or do I tend to rely upon an order to my existence?

Lord, you are sovereign over all situations, and there is nothing that takes place that you have not ordained. Let me be content to rest in your will, being neither anxious nor bitter in whatever befalls me.

Repentance

Q116 – How does the Holy Spirit impart faith to you?

A – By speaking life to me through God's eternal Word, the sacred scriptures, and by effectually drawing me to Christ through repentance.

1 Thessalonians 1:4-6...Romans 10:17...Titus 3:4-6

Q117 – What is repentance?

A – Repentance is the conviction of sin, sorrow over my wicked ways, and consequently turning from sin unto Christ with true resolve to walk in newness of life.

Psalms 51...Ezekiel 14:6...Joel 2:12-13...James 4:7-10

Q118 – Are you able to be saved apart from repentance?

A – No, I cannot be saved without repentance for it is in essence true, saving faith.

Matthew 9:13...Mark 1:15...Luke 13:1-5...Acts 17:30...2 Corinthians 7:9-10

Q119 – How does God the Holy Spirit, then, enable you to repent and believe?

A – By subduing my entire rebellious self to receive the gospel and the effects of the gospel.

2 Timothy 2:24-26...Jeremiah 31:33...1 Thessalonians 1:2-10

Q120 – What is the gospel?

A – Christ Jesus is the gospel, the Son of God come into the world, the light and life of all mankind.

Romans 16:25-26...Galatians 1:11-12...John 1:1-5,14...1 Corinthians 1:30

Questions for Self-Examination and Prayer

Am I receptive to the gospel or capable of any spiritual good apart from the Holy Spirit?

In what way does faith and repentance work together? Does one come before the other?

Of what do I need to repent? What sins do I tend to leave unconfessed?

What does it mean for God to subdue me? Am I willing to be subdued by God in all things?

Lord of my heart, conquer me every day and turn me far from my rebellious self that I might live and not die. Grant me the repentance you require. Find pleasure in me I pray.

Justification

Q121 – What are some of the effects of receiving the gospel?
A – Justification, reconciliation, adoption, sanctification, newness of life, and perseverance of faith.
Romans 5:1-2...Ephesians 1:13...John 11:25-26...2 Corinthians 5:17

Q122 – What is justification?
A – Justification is being made right to God, the grounds for reconciliation, not due to any merit in myself, but due to a gracious declaration on God's part.
Galatians 2:15-16...Genesis 15:6...Romans 1:15-16

Q123 – What does God declare in your justification?
A – That God has forgiven all my sins and that he considers me as righteous in his sight even though I have condemned myself by offending his holiness and glory.
Romans 4:5-8...1 John 1:9...Romans 5:16-17...2 Corinthians 5:19

Q124 – Why would he consider you righteous when you have condemned yourself?
A – Only by the righteousness of Christ Jesus whose sinless blood cleanses my soul and whose perfect obedience merits my life.
Romans 3:21-26...1 Corinthians 5:21...Philippians 3:9-10...1 Peter 3:18

Q125 – Are you then set free from condemnation?
A – Yes. By God's grace, I am made a partaker of Christ's righteous nature, and there is no condemnation for those who are in Christ Jesus.
Romans 8:1-4...2 Peter 1:3-5...Galatians 5:1

Questions for Self-Examination and Prayer

Am I as thankful as I should be for that my sins are forgiven?

If my sins are forgiven and I am made right with God, what is holding me back from a life of spiritual abundance?

Is it not sin when I fail to be thankful for my right standing with God? How do I tend to take his grace for granted?

Father Almighty, let me never take your justifying grace for granted. Fasten me securely to the Rock, for he has secured for me a righteousness which I could never have obtained apart from him.

Adoption and Sanctification

Q126 – What is adoption?

A – Adoption is an act of God's grace whereby he receives me into his family so that I am no longer a child of sin, but rather, a child of God.

Galatians 4:5...Ephesians 1:5...Romans 8:15

Q127 – How does God make you his child when Jesus is his only begotten Son?

A – Only through union with Christ can I become a child of God. He accepts me into his family by the merits of Christ his Son.

John 1:11-13...Romans 8:16...Galatians 3:26

Q128 – What is sanctification?

A – Sanctification is a work of God the Holy Spirit whereby he leads me in the way of truth toward holiness in my entire being with obedience to God's law.

1 Thessalonians 4:3-7...1 Peter 1:2, 15-16...John 17:17...Philippians 2:12-13

Q129 – By what means does the Holy Spirit lead you toward holiness?

A – By the means of the same faith by which I first came to repent and believe.

2 Thessalonians 2:13...Galatians 5:5-6...1 Corinthians 6:11...Jude 20-21...Ephesians 5:25-27...2 Corinthians 5:7

Q130 – Is sanctification natural and automatic for the repentant believer?

A – Natural, yes, in that it is completely compatible with the new life in Christ, but automatic, no, as I must in faith apply further means of grace which God has provided for my sanctification.

2 Peter 1:5-11...1 Corinthians 15:1-2...2 Timothy 2:11...Colossians 1:21-23...Philippians 2:12-13

Questions for Self-Examination and Prayer

Can I even begin to fathom the privilege of adoption into the family of God? What kind of inheritance might be waiting for me?

How does the concept of adoption prove to me that my right standing with God is completely of grace from first to last? Do I make any contribution whatsoever to this place of privilege?

Do I really care to become holy? Is it truly important to me? Am I using the means God has provided to that end?

Father, you have adopted me into your family. I give my life to you. I've done nothing to deserve your favor. Use me for your sacred ends.

The Means of Grace

Q131 – What are the means of grace God has provided for your sanctification?
A – God has provided basic means and casual means. They are both means of receiving, by faith, Christ for salvation.
2 Peter 3:17-18

Q132 – What are basic means of grace?
A – They are the formal means that the Holy Spirit uses to sanctify me, namely, the preached Word, sacraments, and corporate prayer.
Romans 10:14...Acts 2:42...Titus 1:3

Q133 – What are casual means of grace?
A – They are any organic means that the Holy Spirit may use to sanctify me, some examples being scripture study, private prayer, fellowship of the saints, and suffering.
2 Corinthians 4:16-18, 12:9-10...Acts 2:42...James 1:2-4...Philippians 1:3-5...1 John 1:7

Q134 – How is the Word of God to be preached?
A – As the testimony of Christ, boldly and without compromise, with explanation, application, and conviction for the purpose of bringing Christ's glory to bear upon my soul.
2 Corinthians 2:3-5...Revelation 14:6-7...Philippians 1:15-18...1 Peter 1:22-25...Titus 1:9...Acts 8:25...Romans 10:15

Q135 – How does the Holy Spirit use the preached Word to sanctify you?
A – The Holy Spirit applies the preached Word to convict me of sin and to assure me of grace in order that I might draw near to Christ in faith and be saved.
Acts 13:38-39

Questions for Self-Examination and Prayer

Could my spiritual complacency be due to my lack of faithful use the means of grace?

Am I praying as I ought? Am I studying God's Word? Am I serving others? Do I endure suffering with joy?

Do I engage my heart and mind in the regular use of the sacraments? Or do I think them frivolous?

My King, bring Christ to me in all the ways you have ordained for my salvation and forgive me for being so blind to them.

Sacraments

Q136 – What are sacraments?
A – Sacraments are new covenant signs and seals instituted by Christ regarding the salvation offered to us in the gospel.
1 Corinthians 4:1, 10:1-4...Matthew 28:18-20...Luke 22:19-20

Q137 – Is the new covenant a different covenant than the old covenant?
A – No, the new covenant is the same covenant of grace and redemption as the old covenant.
Jeremiah 31:31-34...Exodus 6:5-8...Leviticus 26:44-46...Luke 1:54-55

Q138 – Why, then, do you call it a new covenant?
A – Because Christ, being the great High Priest, has fulfilled the old covenant through his bloodshed and death, having instituted better signs and seals we call sacraments.
2 Corinthians 3:7-11...Hebrews 8:1-8, 13...Ephesians 2:12-13

Q139 – How does the Holy Spirit use the sacraments to sanctify you?
A – The Holy Spirit binds himself to the elements in the sacraments so that, by receiving the elements, I may be assured that I am receiving the Spirit also for the increase of my faith that I might draw near to Christ and be saved.
1 Corinthians 10:16-22, 11:23-25, 12:13

Q140 – How many sacraments do you recognize?
A – There are two sacraments recognized in the new covenant: baptism and the Lord's Supper.
Matthew 28:18-20...Luke 22:19-20

Questions for Self-Examination and Prayer

Do I give thanks as I ought for the blessing of covenant signs?

How does my prayer life reflect my belief that Christ is the High Priest over a more perfect covenant?

Do I truly believe that I have received the Holy Spirit through participation in the sacraments?

Most High God, forgive me for the times I neglect your precious signs and seals and let me use them unto the salvation of my soul. Let nothing you have ordained for my benefit not rest upon this weary soul.

Baptism

Q141 – What is baptism?
A – Baptism is the mark of a christian, a cleansing ritual whereby through the washing with water in the name of the the Lord, I am converted to the faith and counted among Christ's church.
Acts 2:38...Luke 3:3, 21-22...Leviticus 8:1-6...Numbers 19:11-13

Q142 – What is conversion?
A – Conversion is entrance into the new life in Christ, setting me apart to be his disciple.
Acts 3:19...John 3:5-7...Acts 2:41-42

Q143 – What does baptism signify?
A – Baptism signifies spiritual regeneration, cleansing, forgiveness of sins, and the obligation to walk in newness of life.
Titus 3:4-6...Acts 22:16...Romans 6:2-4...Colossians 2:11-13

Q144 – What does baptism seal?
A – Baptism seals unto me the promises of God offered to me in the gospel of Christ to be received by faith.
Ephesians 1:13, 4:30...2 Corinthians 1:21-22...Romans 4:11...Colossians 2:11-12

Q145 – What is meant by a seal?
A – That God has authoritatively marked me with his ownership and given me his Spirit as a deposit guaranteeing the validity of his promises.
Romans 4:11...1 Corinthians 1:21-22...Ephesians 1:13

Questions for Self-Examination and Prayer

Have I been baptized? If not, why not? If so, does it strengthen and chastise me as it should?

Do I realize that, in baptism, following Christ is not an option?

Think about the use of a seal. Do I live as if God owns me?

Am I continuing to believe in the promises held out for me in the symbol and seal of baptism?

Lord, bind me to yourself that the waters of salvation may be to my soul the Spirit of cleansing.

Efficacy of Baptism

Q146 – What does baptism do?

A – Baptism unites me to Christ through the power of the Holy Spirit, assuring me that God is mine and I am his.

Galatians 3:26-27...Romans 6:3-5...1 Corinthians 1:12-13

Q147 – Who is to receive baptism?

A – All who repent and believe must be baptized one time only for the forgiveness of sins.

Mark 1:4...Ephesians 4:4-6

Q148 – Must only those who profess faith be baptized?

A – No. All members of a household of faith must be baptized, including infants and children, even the cognitively impaired.

Acts 2:38-39, 16:14-15, 31-34

Q149 – Why are children of believers also to be baptized?

A – Because children of believers are members of Christ's church by way of the Davidic covenant and therefore rightful heirs to the sign and seal of salvation.

2 Samuel 7:1-16...Acts 2:29-39

Q150 – In what manner does baptism save you?

A – Baptism saves me by virtue of the testimony of the gospel of Christ Jesus.

Mark 16:16...1 Peter 3:21...Titus 3:4-6

Questions for Self-Examination and Prayer

Do I realize that baptism is God's work, not mine?

Do I draw upon my baptism as I ought in my struggle against sin?

Do I rely upon my baptism as a testimony of the gospel of Christ Jesus and his church?

Do I see my baptism as ingrafting me into the body of a larger community?

Gracious Lord, save me and my household, set us apart unto your glory, and count us among your faithful. Bring my thoughts to the waters of salvation for comfort and cleansing when my sins attempt to weigh me down.

The Lord's Supper

Q151 – What is the Lord's Supper?
A – The Lord's Supper is a covenant meal. It is eating the body and blood of the Lord Jesus, not privately, but in a public and corporate manner.
Acts 2:42-46...1 Corinthians 11:20-22

Q152 – Is the Lord's Supper really his body and blood?
A – No, it is really bread and wine.
1 Corinthians 11:23-26

Q153 – Why do you call the Lord's Supper his body and blood?
A – Because the bread represents his body and the wine represents his blood.
Matthew 26:26-28

Q154 – Why do you eat the Lord's Supper?
A – As a memorial to Christ.
Luke 22:19...1 Corinthians 11:24-25

Q155 – Who is allowed to eat the Lord's Supper?
A – The body of Christ, which is called the church.
Colossians 1:24...1 Corinthians 10:16-17

Questions for Self-Examination and Prayer

Do I take the Lord's Supper seriously as a means of grace?

Am I a part of a church that partakes in the Lord's supper frequently as is proper? Or periodically as is improper?

What does it mean to eat as a memorial to Christ? Is this objective or subjective?

Lord, make me eager to come to your table regularly for the spiritual life that you feed to me. I thank you that you renew covenant with me regularly in this gracious meal.

Efficacy of the Lord's Supper

Q156 – What does God require of you who eat the Lord's Supper?
A – That I love God, serve Christ, resist the devil, and repent of sin.
1 Corinthians 6:19-20, 10:14, 11:27-29

Q157 – What are you doing when you eat the Lord's Supper?
A – I am communing with God and the church in Christ.
1 Corinthians 10:16-17

Q158 – What happens when you eat the Lord's Supper?
A – God's wrath passes over me.
1 Thessalonians 5:9...Exodus 12:12-13...1 Corinthians 11:26

Q159 – Why does God's wrath pass over you?
A – Because Christ suffered God's wrath for me when he was crucified, dead, and buried.
1 Peter 2:24...2 Corinthians 5:21...Isaiah 53:5...Romans 3:25

Q160 – What does God do for you when you eat the Lord's Supper?
A – The Holy Spirit strengthens my faith and assurance of salvation.
Luke 22:19...1 Corinthians 11:23-25...John 6:50-51

Questions for Self-Examination and Prayer

Am I willing to repent of my sins? Or do I take the Lord's Supper for granted?

What do I tend to think about during the sacrament? Myself? Or Christ?

Do I think of the Lord's Supper as an individual communion? Or as communion on a larger scale?

How may the Lord's Supper be considered a confession of faith?

Is my partaking of the meal a form of thanksgiving? If so, in what way?

Lord, I thank you that in Christ your wrath falls not upon me, but that through Christ's blood I have gained communion with you and with your redeemed people.

Prayer

Q161 – What is prayer?
A – Prayer is approaching God through the eyes of faith in the name of his Son, Christ Jesus.

Philippians 4:6...Hebrews 4:16...Psalms 5:2-3

Q162 – How does the Holy Spirit use prayer to sanctify you?
A – Prayer facilitates communion with God and draws me near to him, strengthening my faith and assurance of grace.

Jude 20-21...Hebrews 11:6...Romans 8:26-27

Q163 – Why must you not approach God by any other name?
A – Because there is only one mediator between God and man and only one name by which I can be saved, Christ Jesus.

1 Timothy 2:5...Acts 4:12...Hebrews 7:25

Q164 – Do you expect to receive whatever you ask for in prayer?
A – Being that I am a child of God, if I am to pray faithfully according to the name of Christ and in conformity to his revealed will, then I can be sure I will have whatever I ask in due time.

1 John 5:14-15...James 4:2-3...John 14:13-14

Q165 – May you petition God for anything, even if it is not part of his revealed will, and expect to receive it?
A – Being that I am a child of God, if I make any personal desire known to God in a faithful, honorable manner, I can be assured that he will accept my prayer but may not always grant my request for reasons that are known only to himself.

Proverbs 15:29...1 Peter 3:12...2 Corinthians 12:7-9...Matthew 26:39

Questions for Self-Examination and Prayer

Would I consider myself a person of prayer? If not, why?

Can I learn to pray well if I am not saturating myself with God's Word?

Do I tend to pray for my own desires? Or do I focus on God's will?

Lord, teach me to pray. Let me never cease to seek your will.

Model of Prayer

Q166 – Why should you be faithful in praying regularly?
A – Because I am utterly dependent upon God for every good thing, because I need him, and because I can find blessing in no other but him alone.

Mark 14:38...1 Thessalonians 5:17...Psalms 40:17, 55:16-18

Q167 – Are there elements of prayer that are particularly pleasing to God?
A – Yes. I should praise his holy name, confess my sins, give thanks in all things, and offer supplication for myself and others in need.

Colossians 1:9-12...Ephesians 6:18-19...1 Timothy 2:1...Psalms 32:5

Q168 – Why must you be thankful when you pray?
A – Thankfulness is the joyful recognition that God is sovereign and the source of every good thing.

1 Thessalonians:5:16-18...Psalms 100:3-5

Q169 – Must you be thankful even in difficulty?
A – Yes, because there is no difficulty that God has not ordained for his own glory and that he does not use for my good and the good of others.

1 Thessalonians 5:18...Romans 8:28

Q170 – Is there a model of prayer to which you may turn?
A – Yes. Jesus taught his disciples how to pray in what is commonly called the Lord's Prayer.

Matthew 6:5-13

Questions for Self-Examination and Prayer

Am I confessing my sins as I ought? Am I giving thanks in all things?

Do I tend to think about my own needs more than the needs of others? How can I make better intercession for my neighbor?

Do I know how to pray in adversity? Do I handle God's chastisement with humility?

Do I pray well in times of abundance? Or do I grow complacent and forget God's grace?

Lord God Almighty, It is good to come to you in all my weakness knowing that you hear me and will never cast me away. Show me my dependence upon you for every good thing so that I may never forget your grace.

Saving Faith

Q171 – What does it mean to pledge your allegiance to Christ Jesus?

A – It means that because I am not my own, faith is an investment of my entire life and destiny into the hands of the Savior, to follow him with unwavering loyalty.

1 Corinthians 6:19-20...1 Kings 8:60-61...Hebrews 10:23

Q172 – What does it mean to follow Christ with unwavering loyalty?

A – It means that I must deny myself, take up my cross daily, and follow Jesus.

Matthew 16:24-26, 10:38-39...Mark 9:34-38...Romans 12:1

Q173 – Can you not possess saving faith if you do not possess unwavering loyalty?

A – Unwavering loyalty does not imply sinlessness. However, if I ever shirk loyalty in favor of rebellion, then I must confess it as sin and repent lest I forsake the assurance of salvation.

Luke 16:9-15...2 Timothy 2:11-13...Proverbs 28:13...Psalms 32:3-5...Hebrews 10:37-39

Q174 – Is your assurance of salvation not tied, therefore, to saving faith?

A – My assurance of salvation is certainly tied to saving faith unless I am living in willful, unrepentant rebellion against God. Then, of course, I can have no assurance whatsoever that whatever faith I might possess is that of a saving nature.

Deuteronomy 28:15, 66-67...Colossians 2:2-3...Hebrews 10:22-23, 26-27

Q175 – How can faith be otherwise than that of a saving nature?

A – If it is not imparted by God the Holy Spirit, then it is not of a saving nature.

1 Timothy 6:12, 20-21...1 John 2:18-19...Matthew 7:21-23...Acts 5:1-4, 8:13, 20-23

Questions for Self-Examination and Prayer

Have I invested my life and destiny into the hands of the Savior?

Do I ever think that I can possess saving faith without self-denial and suffering?

Am I living in willful, unrepentant rebellion against the authority of God and his law?

Father, give me your Spirit that I might have true allegiance to you alone. Let me have no other gods before you. Break me of every hindrance that tears my loyalty away from you.

Assurance

Q176 – Where, then, would a counterfeit faith be derived?

A – From my own will and imagination, full of pretension.

John 1:13...Isaiah 65:2...Colossians 2:23...2 Peter 3:14-16

Q177 – Is it possible for you to be united to Christ and yet live and die in unbelief?

A – It is certainly possible, which is why I should regularly examine myself that I make my calling and election sure.

1 Peter 1:10...2 Corinthians 13:5...1 Corinthians 10:1-5

Q178 – How can you be united to Christ but not of saving faith?

A – Because union does not necessarily equate to salvation. Rather, when properly applied and not taken for granted, union serves as a catalyst for faith.

Hebrews 3:12-19, 6:4-6...Romans 6:1-5

Q179 – Where, then, is true assurance of saving faith derived?

A – From the presence of the Holy Spirit manifested in inward hope and in the faithful use of the sacraments.

Hebrews 6:11-12, 18-19...2 Thessalonians 2:16-17...Colossians 1:27...2 Timothy 1:12

Q180 – How is hope an assurance of saving faith?

A – Because hope is impossible apart from the presence of the Holy Spirit.

Hebrews 11:1...Romans 15:13...Galatians 5:5

Questions for Self-Examination and Prayer

Do I take my union with Christ for granted?

Where do I find my assurance that I am right with God?

Can I live for myself and still have assurance of salvation?

All Sufficient Lord, convict me of the sins I am prone to hold dear and any pretentiousness that blinds me to the truth. Save me from myself and my self imposed righteousness.

Hope

Q181 – What is hope?

A – Hope is the joyful belief that the promises of God will surely come to pass.

Psalms 33:21-22, 130:7-8...Hebrews 12:1-2

Q182 – In what consists the promises in which you hope?

A – In the manifestation of the glory of God, especially as it consists in my bodily resurrection from the dead and all graces associated with that anticipation.

1 Peter 1:3, 8-9...Romans 5:1-2...1 Corinthians 15:17-19...1 Thessalonians 4:13-14...Acts 23:6

Q183 – How can you be sure that you will be bodily raised from the dead?

A – Because Christ Jesus was bodily raised from the dead, and since I have been united with him in his suffering and death, I will surely be raised with him in everlasting life.

Colossians 3:1...Romans 6:4...2 Timothy 2:10-11

Q184 – What are some of the graces associated with your hope in the bodily resurrection from the dead?

A – Everlasting life, perseverance of faith, and salvation.

Romans 8:24-25, 30...1 Peter 1:8-9...Hebrews 12:1-2...Colossians 3:4...James 1:2...Philippians 1:6

Q185 – Is hope a means of assurance only?

A – No. Hope also motivates me to strive toward love and good deeds knowing that whatever befalls me I am being cared for and brought through life for glorious ends.

Hebrews 10:23-24...Titus 2:11-14...Romans 5:3-4

Questions for Self-Examination and Prayer

What are the things for which I hope most in life?

Does the promise of the resurrection from the dead give me any motivation to live a holy life?

How can I be more conscientious of utilizing hope as an assurance of salvation?

Lord, you have given me reason to hope despite my abundant sins. May you give me a firm grip upon your promises and keep hold of me when I forget to keep hold of you.

Fruits of the Spirit

Q186 – What relationship does hope have with faith?

A – That just as hope is the assurance of faith, faith is the assurance of the things hoped for.

Hebrews 11:1, 13...1 Peter 1:21

Q187 – In what way is faith the assurance of things hoped for?

A – In that through faith, the Holy Spirit bears witness to my spirit that God's promises will not return void.

Philippians 3:20-21...Hebrews 10:21-22...Romans 8:15-17...1 John 5:4-6

Q188 – What is the evidence that the Holy Spirit bears witness to your spirit?

A – The evidence of the Spirit's presence is the fruit that he produces in my life.

Ephesians 2:10...Philippians 2:12-15...Titus 3:5-6...Matthew 7:17-18

Q189 – What is the fruit of the Holy Spirit?

A – Seeking the good of my neighbor and living for God's glory.

Romans 13:10, 15:7...1 Corinthians 10:31

Q190 – What does the fruit of the Spirit look like?

A – Love, joy, peace, patience, kindness, goodness, faithfulness, gentleness, self-control, and any other pure and godly virtue.

Philippians 1:9-11...Galatians 5:22-23...Ephesians 5:8-10...James 3:17

Questions for Self-Examination and Prayer

Which fruit of the Spirit seems to be lacking in my life?

How can something so weak as faith become so crucial to my right standing with God?

What fruit of the Spirit do I most like to see displayed in others?

Lord, produce in me every good fruit by the presence of your Spirit. Create in me a life of virtue for the praise of your glorious grace. May I drink deeply from the spring of life, even at the cost of self-denial.

Virtue

Q191 – But cannot a faithless man also produce good fruits in this life?

A – An unbeliever may produce counterfeit fruits, but apart from faith cannot please God or live for his glory.

Romans 8:7-9...Matthew 7:15-23...3 John 11

Q192 – Can good fruits, then, produce assurance of saving faith?

A – Good fruits in themselves cannot produce assurance, but only the Holy Spirit working through faith unto holiness may produce assurance, thus is faith said to be the assurance of things hoped for.

Romans 6:22...2 Peter 1:2-8...Galatians 5:5-6

Q193 – May you trust in the good fruits of your life as the grounds for your salvation?

A – No, I must trust in Christ alone as the grounds for my salvation, the fruits thereof being the work of God in me.

John 15:4...Acts 4:12...1 Timothy 2:5...Colossians 3:1-25

Q194 – Why, then, should you be expected to exhibit good fruit in your life?

A – Because I am God's workmanship created in Christ Jesus for good works.

Philippians 2:12-13...John 15:5...Ephesians 2:10...Hebrews 13:20-21

Q195 – What happens if you produce bad fruit not in accordance with the Holy Spirit?

A – Then I am worthy of being cut off from Christ and burned in the fire.

Matthew 3:10...Hebrews 6:7-8...John 15:6

Questions for Self-Examination and Prayer

Might I be considered a self-righteous person? Am I basing my righteousness upon my own efforts?

If I am God's workmanship, does my life bear witness to that, or am I in danger of being a fraud?

Do I ever ask myself, in the moment of decision, if my actions bring glory to God? Can I think about this more often?

Heavenly Father, with Christ as my righteousness, may your Holy Spirit produce in me the fruits that your name deserves. I want you to change me into a virtuous disciple of Christ, to live for him, not for myself. Show me what it looks like when your Spirit dwells in me.

Humility

Q196 – What is the greatest virtue?
A – Humility is the greatest virtue.
Micah 6:8...Ecclesiastes 12:13-14...Proverbs 22:4

Q197 – What is humility?
A – Humility is the fear of the Lord, the attitude of my soul which senses complete dependence upon God for every good thing and considers others as more important than myself.
Romans 12:3, 16...Philippians 2:3...Proverbs 9:10...Psalms 128

Q198 – Why is humility rather than love the greatest virtue?
A – Because humility is the root of love, being that love is simply humility in action. This is expounded by Christ in his sermon on the mount.
Philippians 2:1-4...Matthew 5:5-11...Matthew 6:38-48

Q199 – In what manner did Christ exemplify humility?
A – Although very God of very God, he sought not his own will nor did he consider his own life so important that he would not lay it down as a ransom for sinners.
Philippians 2:8...1 Peter 3:17-18...Luke 22:27...John 8:50

Q200 – Can you be saved apart from humility?
A – No, because God opposes the proud but gives grace to the humble. Humility is the condition of saving faith.
James 4:6-10...1 Peter 5:5-7...Luke 18:13-14

Questions for Self-Examination and Prayer

Do I ever consider that God is humble yet still demands loyalty? Can I display humility in my own stations of life?

Do I fear God like I should? How would my life be different if I feared him more?

Am I willing to be humbled by God, even if it brings a measure of suffering to my life?

What relationship does humility have with self-sacrifice? Must they always go hand in hand?

Gracious God, praise be to Christ who humbled himself to the death for my sins. May I learn to do likewise. Make me low that I might be lifted up by your saving hand.

Perseverance

Q201 – What is the perseverance of faith?
A – Perseverance is a grace of God whereby he keeps me in the faith of Christ from the time of my conversion until the end of my earthly life.
Philippians 1:6...Hebrews 12:2...1 Peter 1:3-5...2 Timothy 1:12

Q202 – Can you ever lose or forfeit your faith?
A – By sin I may weaken my faith, by unbelief I may disprove my faith, but saving faith may never be lost or forfeited because it is a gift of God that he intends I keep.
Ephesians 2:8...John 6:38-40...Mark 4:13-20...1 Corinthians 15:1-2

Q203 – How does God keep you in the faith?
A – By his power to do so in accordance with his faithful promises.
2 Peter 3:9...Hebrews 11:39-40...Ephesians 1:13-14...2 Corinthians 5:5...Romans 1:16...2 Timothy 1:12

Q204 – How does perseverance come to pass?
A – God the Father has predestined me unto everlasting life, God the Son has purchased my pardon by his blood, and God the Holy Spirit made me alive and keeps me in Christ until the day of salvation.
Ephesians 1:3-7, 13,14...1 Peter 3:18

Q205 – How can you be sure that God will not abandon you?
A – Because he who began a good work in me will be faithful to complete it.
Philippians 1:6...Romans 8:37-39...Hebrews 13:5

Questions for Self-Examination and Prayer

How does knowing the doctrine of perseverance affect my assurance of salvation?

How might I misunderstand this doctrine so that I take God's grace for granted?

How has God shown me his faithfulness in the past? How has he worked to sanctify me, even in my foolishness and sin?

How might my understanding of perseverance relate to my understanding of the sacraments?

Sovereign Lord, I thank you that my eternal destiny is in your hands, not mine, for I am your workmanship.

Nature of Salvation

Q206 – What is salvation?
A – Salvation is the experience of being rescued from danger, especially sin, death, and hell.

2 Samuel 22:2-7...Matthew 1:21...1 Corinthians 15:1-2

Q207 – How is salvation manifest?
A – Salvation is manifest in three parts: past, present, and future.

1 Peter 1:3-9...1 Corinthians 15:1-2

Q208 – How is salvation manifest in the past?
A – When God called me out of darkness and brought me into his marvelous light, making me alive in Christ by faith, and justifying me.

2 Timothy 1:8-9...1 Peter 2:9, 3:18...Ephesians 2:4-6...Colossians 2:13...Titus 3:4-7...1 Corinthians 6:11...Romans 5:1

Q209 – How is salvation manifest in the present?
A – When God works in my life unto holiness, conforming me to the likeness of Jesus.

Philippians 2:13...Ephesians 3:19-20...Hebrews 2:11, 10:14...1 Peter 1:8-9...Romans 6:22...1 Corinthians 1:18, 7:1...2 Corinthians 6:2...1 Thessalonians 4:3-4...2 Thessalonians 2:13...Titus 2:11-12

Q210 – How is salvation manifest in the future?
A – When God will raise me from the dead unto sinless perfection. This is the final and fullest realization of the salvation experience and rightly called salvation itself.

Titus 2:13...Hebrews 9:27-28, 11:39-40...1 John 3:2...1 Corinthians 15:20-26...1 Thessalonians 1:9-10...Ephesians 1:13-14...Philippians 3:10-12...Romans 5:8-9, 13:11...1 Peter 1:4-5, 13

Questions for Self-Examination and Prayer

Do I understand that I am a child of light? Why would I want to return to the darkness?

How much do I desire to be made in the image of Christ? Am I willing enough so that it hurts?

Must I live in a state of uncertainty? What promises can I hold on to that this tumultuous life will end in liberation and perfection?

Merciful God, hold me close to you from the first to the last. Let me never give up hoping for your salvation nor striving to obtain it.

Sphere Authority

Q211 – What are the spheres of life in which authority exists?
A – There exist three spheres of authority: the family, the church, and the state, each distinct in purpose and function.
Matthew 28:18-20...Romans 13:1...Genesis 1:27-28

Q212 – Of what does the jurisdiction of the family consist?
A – The jurisdiction of the family consists of the propagation of human life, nurture, education, culture, health, tradition, religion, vocation, and the right to secure these blessings.
Genesis 1:27-28...Genesis 4:16-22...Joshua 24:15

Q213 – Who is the primary authority in the family structure?
A – The father is the primary authority and head over the family structure and consequently held accountable by God for the quality of his household economy.
1 Samuel 3:11-14...1 Corinthians 11:3...Genesis 7:1, 18:17-19

Q214 – Of what does the jurisdiction of the church consist?
A – The jurisdiction of the church consists of rightly handling the keys of the kingdom of God which is Word and sacrament, apart from which there is no ordinary possibility of salvation.
Matthew 16:18-19...1 Timothy 3:15...1 Corinthians 11:27-29

Q215 – Who is the primary authority of the church?
A – Christ himself, as head of the church, is the primary authority of the church.
Colossians 1:18...Ephesians 1:22-23, 5:23

Questions for Self-Examination and Prayer

Of the family, the church, and the state, which is the most important to society?

Is my household submitting to the father as it ought? Is it submitting to God's law?

Is my household submitting to the authority of the church as it ought, with Christ as the head?

How close of a relationship should the family have with the church?

Holy Lord, this world is full of brokenness and destruction, especially in the family. Sanctify my household that we may be a family of light shining in the darkness of this world, confessing our sins together.

Nature of the Church

Q216 – Who is the church?
A – The church is those who are the Israel of God, also called the body and bride of Christ, with whom he covenants and communes in Heaven and on earth.
Galatians 6:15-16...Romans 14:17-18...Ephesians 2:19-21...Colossians 1:24...Acts 2:40-47...Psalm 95:6-7

Q217 – How should the church be distinguished from the world?
A – The church is entrusted with the Word of God for the pursuit of holiness and love between brethren.
Romans 12:2...1 Corinthians 1:21-24, 2:11-13...James 1:27, 4:4...2 Peter 1:3-4...1 John 2:16, 4:4-7

Q218 – How is the church manifest?
A – The church is manifest as the principle expression of God's kingdom, both militant and triumphant.
1 Corinthians 4:17-20, 6:9-11...Mark 1:15...Daniel 2:44

Q219 – Who are the church militant?
A – The church militant are the visible, baptized saints throughout the earth who gather to hear God's Word and commune together, battling against the world, the flesh, and the devil.
Matthew 16:18...Acts 2:41-42

Q220 – How are the church militant manifest?
A – The church militant are manifest in two ways: the organic and the ecclesiastical.
Matthew 18:15-33...Ephesians 2:19-21

Questions for Self-Examination and Prayer

As a Christian, in what ways do I stand alone before God?

As a Christian, in what ways do I stand as part of a body? Where should my identity be found?

Do I think of myself as being part of the true Israel? As part of the community created from God's covenant with Abraham?

Lord, may I die to myself. Let me find my true identity in Christ, as part of his body from which I draw my sustenance. May the body of Christ be unto me a safe haven, a refuge from the war that wages in my soul.

The Church Organic

Q221 – What is the organic aspect of the church?
A – The organic aspect of the church consists in living life together and growing as a family of believers.
Galatians 6:10...Ephesians 2:19

Q222 – How is life together manifest?
A – Through Christ-centered community exemplified by gathering together, bearing each other's burdens, and humbling ourselves in faith and practice.
Galatians 6:2...Titus 2:1-9...Acts 4:32-35...Revelation 1:4

Q223 – What is the purpose of gathering?
A – Gathering is the physical coming together in particular times and places to meet with God and worship him corporately around Word and sacrament.
Hebrews 10:24-25...Acts 2:46...1 Corinthians 11:18, 14:26

Q224 – When does the church gather to meet with God and worship him together?
A – The Lord's Day, being the first day of the week, is the primary occasion to gather for corporate worship.
Acts 20:7...1 Corinthians 16:2...Revelation 1:10

Q225 – Why should the Lord's Day be set aside for corporate worship?
A – Because the first day of the week is the day of Christ's resurrection and the example set by the apostolic church.
Matthew 28:1...Mark 16:1-6...Acts 20:7

Questions for Self-Examination and Prayer

How important is it to me to meet together with the Christians for worship? Is it as important as it should be? Do I neglect the gatherings?

How important is it for me to meet together with Christians outside of the worship service? Am I seeking to meet the needs of others as I ought? Am I seeking to be edified through fellowship? Do I desire to be kept accountable in my lifestyle and behavior?

Blessed Father, may you place saints in my life who can challenge me in the faith to pursue love and good deeds and with whom I can share in the trials and joys of life.

Church Government

Q226 – What is the ecclesiastical aspect of the church militant?
A – The ecclesiastical aspect of the church is the institutional manifestation as a body politic.
1 Peter 2:9...Matthew 18:15-18...Revelation 1:5-6, 5:9-10...Hebrews 13:7,17

Q227 – How does Christ enforce his authority when he is not physically present to govern his body?
A – Christ governs through the use of certain men who are called to be overseers.
1 Peter 5:2...Matthew 28:18...Ephesians 4:11-12...Acts 20:28

Q228 – What is the role of overseers?
A – The overseers are ministers who are to shepherd the church, keep sound doctrine, preach and teach God's Word, administer sacraments, pray for the church militant, and maintain godly order in the gatherings.
Titus 2:1...James 5:14...2 Timothy 4:2...Acts 6:2-4, 20:28-29

Q229 – On what criteria are overseers elected?
A – Overseers must be wise, virtuous, well-experienced in the faith, tested and proven, and willing to lead and govern.
1 Peter 5:2-3...2 Timothy 2:2...1 Timothy 3:1-7

Q230 – When did Christ first delegate his authority?
A – Christ delegated his authority to his apostles when he vested in them the keys of the kingdom of heaven and when he commissioned them shortly before his ascension.
Matthew 28:19-20...Matthew 16:19

Questions for Self-Examination and Prayer

Do I support the office of overseer within the church? Am I promoting wise and godly men for this office?

Am I thankful for the order and structure God has ordained for the church? Or do I seek to usurp the order?

How should the office of overseer serve as a motivation for all men to pursue holiness? Is holy living only for a select few? Or for men only?

My Lord and King, may you raise up godly, faithful, and courageous men to lead your church. May you raise up men willing to die to themselves and pursue the holiness that is required of your people.

Authority of Overseers

Q231 – What are the keys of the kingdom of heaven?
A – The keys are the power to grant entry into the life in Christ and the power to close off entry into the life in Christ, meaning the power of Word and sacrament.
Matthew 16:19...Acts 3:5-7

Q232 – How does the Word and sacrament grant or close off entry into the life of Christ?
A – By the Spirit of God, the Word preached has the power to awaken belief or condemn unbelief, and the sacraments work likewise.
1 Corinthians 4:2-4...Romans 1:16...1 Corinthians 11:27-29

Q233 – Are all overseers given the same power as that of the apostles?
A – Overseers are not apostles but only exercise authority in the governance of the church body as long as they remain in submission to the apostolic teachings of Christ.
1 Corinthians 9:1-2...2 Corinthians 12:2...Ephesians 4:11-12...Acts 2:42-43...Luke 6:13-16

Q234 – What is apostolic teaching?
A – Apostolic teaching is the teaching of Christ expounded by the apostles and propagated throughout the church in the first generation after his ascension.
Jude 17,18...2 Peter 3:1-3...Acts 1:1-3, 2:42...Ephesians 2:19-20...Galatians 2:8-9

Q235 – Wherein consists the respect offered up to the overseers?
A – Overseers, though fallible, are to be respected for the office they hold, but only so far as they fear God. Respect for the office does not transcend tyrannical behaviors.
1 Corinthians 9:13-14...1 Peter 5:3...1 Timothy 5:17...Acts 20:28-30...Hebrews 13:7

Questions for Self-Examination and Prayer

Am I willing to submit to the proper authorities within the church?

Do I pray for the overseers as I ought? Or do I find myself complaining about them?

How can I respect my overseers while at the same time keeping them accountable to God's Word?

Lord of Light, give me wisdom to submit to those whom you have placed over me, and may you bind them to your Word so that you might keep your people protected under their care.

The Purpose of the Church

Q236 – Will all the church militant be saved?

A – No. The church militant is a mixture of both faithful and faithless, humble and pretentious, wheat and tares.

2 Corinthians 11:13-15...Matthew 13:24-30...1 Peter 4:17...Philippians 1:18...Matthew 7:21

Q237 – Who are the church triumphant?

A – The church triumphant are the saints who have died and have gone into the presence of God, waiting for the resurrection of the body and still holding communion with those on earth.

Revelation 20:4...1 Thessalonians 3:13...Hebrews 11:39-40

Q238 – Will all the church triumphant be saved?

A – Yes. They have passed the test and are now in the glorious presence of God.

2 Corinthians 5:6-8...Revelation 7:9...Philippians 1:23

Q239 – What is the chief end of the church?

A – To be holy, set apart unto God's glory, bearing fruit for Christ's sake having been restored to rule over God's earthly creation as prophets, priests, and kings.

Ephesians 5:25-27...Philippians 2:14-15...1 Peter 1:15-16...John 15:8...Revelation 1:5-6

Q240 – Is there such a thing as a false church?

A – A false church is no church at all, but has abandoned the apostolic teachings regarding the faith and practice of the gospel.

Revelation 19:20...Matthew 24:24...Galatians 1:6-9...2 Corinthians 11:12-14

Questions for Self-Examination and Prayer

Is it a frightening thought that unbelief crops up among the belief? Do I have the wisdom to distinguish between the two?

What would it be like to be sanctified with God in Heaven yet still unsatisfied, longing for the time in which the body will be raised up unto perfection?

Do I think the church is being faithful to its chief end? What can I do in my life to help it succeed?

Most Holy Lord, show me any way in me that is false that I might not disown you. Have mercy upon this sinner and use me for the building up of your church.

Offices of Christ

Q241 – What are the marks of the church?
A – Faithful apostolic teaching, faithful use of the sacraments, and faithful discipline despite imperfections.
Acts 2:42-47

Q242 – On what basis may man be rightly restored to the offices of prophet, priest, and king?
A – On the basis that Christ Jesus has prepared those offices for me by executing them himself on my behalf.
Colossians 1:13-14...Revelation 1:6, 5:9-10

Q243 – How does Christ execute the office of prophet?
A – By revealing to me his works and will through his apostles.
Matthew 5:17, 21:46...Hebrews 1:1-2...Romans 1:4-6...Galatians 1:11-12...Ephesians 2:20...Luke 24:44-45

Q244 – How does Christ execute the office of priest?
A – By making intercession for me in his sacrificial atonement as well as in his resurrection and ascension, being seated at the right hand of the Father in glory.
Hebrews 3:1-3. 7:24-26...Revelation 1:5

Q245 – How does Christ execute the office of king?
A – By ruling and defending me, by establishing justice, and by leading me into battle against the forces of darkness.
Revelation 17:14...Ephesians 6:10-13...Matthew 2:1-2

Questions for Self-Examination and Prayer

How might I function as a prophet? What can I do to make Christ known?

Do I see myself as a king? What does that mean for me in the my own station of life?

What type of priestly work can I do for Christ? Can I serve as a priest in my lowly position? Who can I intercede for? Who can I sacrifice for? Who can I serve?

Lord, thanks be to Christ, my Prophet, Priest, and King, by whom I am redeemed and restored unto a proper place upon this earth. May his light shine in and through me as I seek to live humbly and faithfully before you and the watching world.

Functions of the State

Q246 – Of what does the jurisdiction of the state consist?
A – The jurisdiction of the state consists of ensuring justice on behalf of the commonwealth for the sake of peace within the commonwealth.
Proverbs 29:4, 16:12...Romans 13:3-4

Q247 – Is the state, then, obligated to submit to God in all matters of justice?
A – Yes, because there is no authority except that which God has established, and all authority in Heaven and on earth has been given to Christ Jesus.
Romans 13:1...Matthew 28:18...1 Chronicles 29:10-12...Revelation 1:5

Q248 – May the state interfere in the jurisdictions of the church and family?
A – No, because it is unjust for any proper sphere of jurisdiction to interfere with the rightly vested powers of any other jurisdiction whether it be the family, the church, or the state.
Romans 13:7...Matthew 22:21...Joshua 24:14-20

Q249 – What course of action may be taken when one God-ordained sphere attempts to infringe upon another God-ordained sphere?
A – The violated party may humbly protest and if need be resist, nullify, or disobey any tyranny imposed by the unjust party.
Acts 5:27-29...Daniel 3:16-18...Esther 3:2-3

Q250 – What measure of respect ought to be given to the state?
A – God requires that I honor all proper governing authorities, to pray for them, and to submit to them as a matter of conscience.
1 Peter 2:13-14...Titus 3:1...Romans 12:17-19, 13:4-5

Questions for Self-Examination and Prayer

Is the state always my friend? What are some instances in which I ought not to comply with state regulations?

Why is it dangerous for the church to impose its will on the state?

Do I have a tendency to honor the state more than God?

Do I have a tendency to listen to the state's counsel over God's counsel?

Lord God, holy and just, let the idols of my heart crumble, and may those who govern me honor you, and, for the sake of your Kingdom and righteousness, may you crush them if they rise up against you.

The Forces of Darkness

Q251 – What must you do when your conscience is violated by the dictates of an authoritative figure?
A – My conscience ought to be bound to the Word of God, and therefore my allegiance ought to be given to Christ before any earthly power, even upon the pain of suffering.
Luke 4:5-7...Matthew 4:8-11, 12:25-26...Daniel 10:13...2 Corinthians 4:4...Colossians 1:13...John 12:31...1 John 5:19

Q252 – What existing powers are in competition with the authoritative power of Christ in this world?
A – The kingdom of darkness, consisting of the devil and his army, despises Christ and his Kingdom and has been seeking to usurp Christ's power and authority since the creation of man.
Revelation 2:13, 16:10-11, 19:19...Colossians 1:13...2 Thessalonians 2:3-4...Genesis 3:1...Ephesians 6:12

Q253 – How does the kingdom of darkness seek to usurp the Kingdom of Christ?
A – The forces of darkness are active in the family and the church as well as the state, covenanting with wicked men and together conspiring against Christ and all that is good and right.
Psalms 2:1-3, 10, 64:1-6...John 11:47-53...Luke 22:2-4...Acts 9:23-25

Q254 – From where do the forces of darkness derive their authority?
A – Being that they are in rebellion, there is no authority given to the forces of darkness except that which God allows them to pretend for a time, for his own purposes, as they attempt to seduce both the nations and the Kingdom of Christ.
Revelation 17:17

Q255 – Is there reason to fear the forces of darkness?
A – There is no reason to fear any besides the one who is able to cast both body and soul into hell, that being the Most High God alone. Nevertheless, I should stand on guard against all evil kingdoms and beware of the schemes of wicked men aimed at

the destruction of the righteous.

Matthew 10:28...Colossians 1:13

Questions for Self-Examination and Prayer

Do I close my eyes to the conspiracies of darkness? Do I turn a deaf ear to the wake-up calls?

Am I overly caught up in current events? Have I been deceived by the narrative? Do I fear needlessly?

Does my christian worldview include the reality of God's providence? Does it include the reality of conspiracy?

Father of Light, protect your church from the powers of evil, and prepare us for battle in mind and heart. Open my eyes to the schemes of wicked men that I might not be deceived, and be gracious to me when I am blind.

Judgment

Q256 – Where is the kingdom of Christ to be found?
A – Christ's kingdom, being a kingdom of light, is found in his one holy, catholic, and apostolic church.

2 Peter 1:1-11, 3:1-2..Ephesians 4:1-6, 11-13...1 Peter 2:9...John 18:36...1 Thessalonians 5:4-5

Q257 – What is the extent of Christ's kingdom?
A – Christ has promised to build his church atop the ruins of the kingdom of darkness, and therefore Christ's kingdom will be established in every place that his Word is preached and received.

Matthew 16:18...Ephesians 5:8-11...Mark 16:15-16, 20... Revelation 11:15

Q258 – What results should you expect regarding the battle between the forces of darkness and the church of Christ Jesus?
A – Being that Christ has already declared victory over the evil one by virtue of his resurrection and ascension, I should expect complete victory for Christ on the final day of judgment.

1 Corinthians 15:54-58...Mark 16:19-20...Revelation 20:10

Q259 – Of what does the final day of judgment consist?
A – The day of judgment consists of Christ's final victory over the forces of darkness, his bodily return, the destruction of the wicked, the bodily resurrection from the dead of the righteous, and the inauguration of the everlasting kingdom of God.

2 Thessalonians 1:7-10...1 Corinthians 15:24-25...Revelation 20:11-15, 21:1-4

Q260 – How, then, can you do battle against the wickedness in the world until the final day?
A – I must deny myself, take up my cross daily, and follow Jesus.

Ephesians 6:10-18...Matthew 16:24

Questions for Self-Examination and Prayer

How would my life be different if I expected God to win the battle against the forces of darkness? Where is the victory ultimately won?

How is prayer a weapon against evil? How might the world change if I would take up my cross daily? What if I prayed faithfully?

Sovereign Lord, the victory is yours. Forgive me for not fighting with more boldness and faith. Make me your servant and a soldier in the battle over life and death, good and evil, and right and wrong. You alone are worthy of all glory, honor, and praise, dominion and authority forever and ever.